REFLECTIONS ON DEATH

Printed in the United States of America
First Printing, 2025

ISBN: 979-8-9997941-0-9

John A. Kessler
611 E. Hill Road #205D
Southbury, CT 06488

REFLECTIONS ON DEATH

*A collection of writings
to comfort and smooth your
journey through the
loss of a loved one*

John A. Kessler

In loving memory of my wife Marion, who has now begun the journey down her new road.

With gratitude to Fr. Bill Considine and Fr. Don LaSalle at Lourdes in Litchfield, who are my pillars of strength.

To Alison, Charlie, Fran, and Lori, who give me support.

For the help of Paula and Judy, who helped me finish this work.

INTRODUCTION

Let me propose that our life is a musical production, or more specifically put, "OUR SYMPHONY OF LIFE," composed by a higher authority and conducted by ourselves.

Death is not an isolated event but rather another movement in the rhythm of our life. Depending on your beliefs, or for other personal reasons, it is only the next step on our journey into an anticipated future.

So, take hold of the fact that death is a natural next step, a movement in your Symphony, and not the dark and foreboding shadow lurking in your future.

THE ROAD OF LIFE

At our birth each of us is given a road to travel on. We have no idea where this road will lead nor how long it will take to arrive at some unknown destination.

In the early years of life our journey on this road is usually guided by a parent or another close adult. Needless to say that these early guided years are out of our control and "we are just along for the ride".

At some point we break the bonds of care and embark on our own to continue and finish the journey. It's this journey now that will present the many challenges, successes and failures in store for us. There will be good times, bad times and unfortunately ill health times. When these events happen is uncertain and certainly unplanned for.

But there comes that point where we first encounter our mortality through the death of a loved one. Now we have hit the one unavoidable bump in our road which is unexpected and shocking. Until now we have always been able to fix or find a solution to any problem.

Now what? How do I handle this one unavoidable roadblock which I cannot detour around. Is this the end of my journey down my road of life? But wait, if you gather yourself and think calmly about this development, you will slowly begin to understand that there are a number of tools you can use to find ways around this impenetrable wall.

These aids or tools are: friends, prayer, grief, memories and family. What a powerful arsenal you actually have at your disposal. So here you are, not at the end of your road, but simply on your new road less traveled.

"Death ends a life, not a relationship. All the love you created is still here. All the memories are still there. You live in the hearts of everyone you have touched and nurtured while you were here."

– **Mitch Albom**

AWAITING

For many, the loss of a loved one may begin long before the actual loss itself. Due to disease or illness you may have become a caregiver months or years before the actual departure. During that time you have witnessed their pain and suffering. Unknowingly you have begun what we know as "Anticipatory Grief".

This is a more silent form of grief but is no less devastating than the grief you will experience at the moment of actual loss. It tends to infect your mind and heart in a slowly invasive way.

It is such a silent assault on your total being that it quietly prepares you for the loss in a way that may also take away or limit the shock of the actual loss.

It is such a silent attacker that it creates as much damage as a serious illness. It may also leave you without emotion at the actual moment of a loss. It can silently drain you of the ability to process loss in a more normal fashion.

But take heart. In the end the human spirit will take hold and restore a sense of normalcy to your grieving process.

DEATH

It came to visit this day
An unwelcome guest at best
I tried not to notice it
For surely this was a test

Indeed it was known to me
That one day would appear
This frightening specter
Who would soon evoke a tear

The first thought that came to me
Was the silent urge to resist
But soon it became evident
That he would insist

There would be no way to change
This moment that would take place
Perhaps the better course to take
Would be to accept it with grace

In life there are so many things
Which we can control
But the one event closed to us
Is the taking of the soul

THE ARRIVAL

My slumber awakened with a chill,
So disturbing that I stepped to the sill

Nothing seemed to be amiss
But my being would not dismiss

The peaceful night had fled away
Replaced by only a gentle sway

A voice said gently, death is here,
But you need not fear.
For I come for the one you hold dear

Worry not my friend, for your loved one
Has found peace,and so will you,
The pain will slowly cease.

"Goodbyes are only for those who love with their eyes, because for those who love with Heart and soul, there is no such thing as separation."

– Rumi

THE DEPARTURE

Silently as a summer breeze
A soul slipped away

Wordlessly it left, no clue
For it to betray

Where had it gone, only
God could say

My mind swirled endlessly
Questions with no answer today

And then a light shone brightly
As clouds parted away

I understood at last
Why this soul had slipped away

"There is a sacredness in tears; they are not the mark of weakness, but of power."

— Washington Irving

IT'S ALRIGHT TO CRY

When your heart is full of happiness or grief it needs to overflow and does so through your tears. Many consider tears or the simple act of crying to be symbols of weakness. But, the act of producing tears is a sign of strength and emotional well being. If you could not shed tears, how then would you visibly express an emotion?

As a youth many, especially boys, are cautioned not to cry or they will be labeled as a sissy or worse. As we grow and mature, women especially learn how to express their emotions through the shedding of tears. Men to the contrary remain stuck in the male "Macho" attitude.

Never fear nor feel ashamed if you shed tears, they are the fountain of your heart. As Ernst Moritz Arndt stated, "Tears are the messengers of true love."

"The life of the dead is placed in the Memory of the living."

– Marcus Tallius Cicero

BEAUTIFUL MEMORIES

My mind wandered aimlessly
Like a ship bobbing in the sea

Searching for a port to slip into
But for the mist I could not see

And then like a starburst
The mist was swept away

At that very moment
Memories saved the day

They cleared away the shadows
And kept this darkness at bay

For memories are important
You want them to stay

They keep that person alive
Who loved you in every way

"Grieving allows us to heal, to remember with love rather than with pain. It is a sorting process. One by one you let go of things that are gone and you mourn for them. One by one you take hold of the things that have become a part of who you are and build again."

– Rachael Naomi Remen

GRIEF FOREVER

I Grieve today, will it be forever
Will this burden never end

How much pain must I carry
Is it for a lifetime, will it tarry

But grief is not a penalty to punish
It is the will to carry on

For if I do not grieve my loss
How else will the pain be gone

Yes, grief is forever, this is true
You will be more at peace through and through

MIXED EMOTIONS

I have lost a dear one
Not sure how I feel
They are gone and my
mind is blank

Cannot say if this is real
Without even a fond
goodbye, gone from me
in the blink of an eye

My mind cannot fathom
this empty space. I'm expected
to accept it with quiet grace

But who's to say how I should feel
For in the end I know it is real

LONELINESS

Like a statue I feel alone
Locked in a place like a stone

There no longer is a hand to hold
Or countless memories to be told

The noise and clatter all gone away
Perhaps death now holds it all at bay

The curtain seems to have been drawn
Will it open again with the new dawn

I wait for sound to reappear
Perhaps then loneliness will disappear

YOUR STORY

We never know when a special story is going to be told, and so often we do not recognize one when it is. And so this could be your story.

It began in the warmth of spring when nature itself was awakening to New Life. You may not have realized it but a new life for you was born that day. Like all new things it began to grow slowly with only subtle hints of what it might grow to be.

It took form in quiet moments with serious and interesting conversation coupled with laughter. Soon it became part of your days and communication blossomed.

Before long summer was upon you and with it came the first feelings of how deep and true the relationship was becoming. You began the process of learning about each other.

Something special then happened when you became aware of the deep respect you had for each other. Your hearts and minds joined in common goals as you began to fully understand and appreciate each other as unique persons with specific needs and identities.

Then Fall was upon you and your bond matured and grew deeper. You saw more clearly how much you could grow together and the future became more exciting. The prospect of living your lives together and helping each other grow became part of your very being.

There will always be so much to do together, so much to talk about. More perhaps than can be handled in a lifetime. But that is what a strong relationship is all about, continuing to learn, grow and mature.

So, this could be your story, the greatest story ever told!

"Guilt is perhaps the most painful Companion to death."

– Elizabeth Kubler Ross

THE BURDEN AND JOY OF GUILT

I have been coming to this place for the last five years since the passing of my dear one. This loss and a self imposed sense of guilt continues to bring me here.

Did I do enough for her, was I present as much as I could have been? Was I as comforting as I could have been? These and other emotions have crowded out more sensible thoughts Coming here gives me hope that a new day will also be the start of a renewed life for me.

I stand on the shore in the dark of night, my spirit just as dark, gazing at the horizon. Suddenly, a golden sliver of light slowly breaks the darkness and in a deliberate and measured way the golden light spreads like a carpet of jewels across the water. Now complete, a new day has dawned, but sadly, nothing changed for me.

I turn and walk down the beach still carrying my burden. As I walk, I see a woman sitting in her chair also taking in the dawn. I have never encountered anybody before, so I stop to bid good morning. She smiles and acknowledges my greeting. A friendly conversation ensues and I find that like myself she is here for much the same reason as I. She explains that many years ago her father lost his life at this spot saving her life from the sea As she grew up she began to develop a sense of guilt over his sacrifice.

However, unlike myself, she came to terms with her grief and guilt. She explained that grief became a valuable tool in understanding what had taken place. In an extraordinary act of love her father had chosen her life over his own. It was the greatest gift he had to give and it was freely given. Now she understands and comes here not so much to grieve but to celebrate his passing. Like a flash of lightning, it hits me that my Guilt is not providing me with anything positive but rather is stopping me from celebrating a beautiful life. I then bid goodbye and continued my walk with a different perspective on my life.

I often return to my beach and I reflect on all of my wonderful memories instead of my destructive guilt. Strangely, I never again saw the woman who changed my life. I have a very strong sense that my beautiful love sent this messenger to me for that chance encounter.

You may view this short story as a lovely fairy tale, but think carefully for a moment, how do you bear your grief? Has it been a heavy burden, crippling at times, or a constant distraction keeping you from the joyful life your loved one would want for you. We all may not encounter an unknown messenger, but be assured, there will be human messengers in the guise of friends, family, clergy and others who are willing to be your secret guides sent by your loved one.

"To Die, To Sleep. To Sleep, Perchance To Dream – Ay–There's The Rub. For In This Sleep Of Death What Dreams May Come."

– William Shakespeare

IN THE DARK OF NIGHT I DREAM

Day has slipped away
Night has taken its place
Daylight which lifted my spirit
Is now replaced by foreboding dark

Fitfully I slip into slumber
Escaping the darkness,
Attacked by dreams of
That which departed my life

The memories now battle
My dark dreams
And lift the sorrow away

I take heart in knowing
Despite this raging battle within
The darkest hour precedes the dawn

SIGNS

When traveling, they show us the way
When lost, keep us from going astray

Mileposts tell us how far to go
Others show us where to stay

In the Melody of life when we feel lost
Signs remind us of a life lost

They were sent to comfort us
And soothe our painful grief

They remind us in a special way
Our loved one still has much to say

They really have not left us
But are truly still here

And signs are the way
They continue to share

AN ENDURING CONVERSATION

You must not remain silent
When a loved one has gone

Talk to your special person
For they are still here

Speak of the things you wish
To share, knowing that they still care

They will listen to you with
An open heart
All they need is for you to start

Life goes on that is for certain
Let them in, just raise the curtain

"The pain passes, but the beauty remains."

– Pierre Auguste Renoir

ALIVE INSIDE

So often after the loss of a loved one you are told or have heard it said, "Time heals all wounds"

"Time to get on with your life"

"Your loved one is in a better place"

These age-old and well intentioned platitudes are meant to make you feel better, perk up your spirits and generally cheer you up. How misleading they all are.

Time is not a great healer but more often a slow and questionable recovery process. What most people refer to with this statement are the wounds to your heart and your mind. As we have come to learn there is no medicine or bandage that will relieve the pain or cure these wounds. Yes, eventually time will slowly join you on your walk of grief but time alone is not the magic cure that it is portrayed to be.

As for time to get on with your life, who is to say when we are ready to move ahead. For some, that time will come relatively quickly and for others it may take longer. So you see, it may not be your right time, but your heart will tell you when the time is right for you.

The last statement about your loved one being in a better place is the most difficult to address. For a variety of reasons such as an incurable illness, you may want your loved one to be relieved of their pain and suffering and frankly you might feel any place is better than here where they are suffering. Our human mind cannot readily accept the idea that anywhere other than with you is a better place. But being human, and perhaps a little selfish, we want our loved one to be with us as long as possible. Can it be that in the early stages of a loss we cannot think clearly enough to grasp the idea, that yes, given some time we will move on with life, and most importantly, our loved one will be in a better place, alive inside our heart and memory.

SPEAK TO ME

In my deepest silence
I yearn for you to speak to me

When life becomes most challenging
I listen for you to speak to me

When I am troubled and sad
I pray for you to speak to me

When all else fails and I lose heart
I cry for you to speak to me

As I tread the difficult path of life
I know you will speak to me

"You gave me a forever within the numbered days."

– John Green

YOU ARE GONE BUT HAVE NOT LEFT ME

I know for certain that you are gone
But I know as well that you have not left

For you are there each day in many ways
Not visible to see but there anyway

Your smile reminds me how you lit my life
Your laughter echoes throughout my soul

Your touch warms my heart
Your voice is a gentle melody of peace

Yes, you are gone but you have not left me

WHY DID YOU DO THIS TO ME?

Often, when we suffer the loss of a loved one, not only sorrow and grief affect us, but many times so does anger.

We get frustrated and cannot help ourselves from experiencing anger. We are hurt, feel helpless and vent our hurt through anger. We start to think that death somehow is striking out at us through our loved one and we just plain get mad!

But take heart, this a brief emotional response that will quickly pass. Always remember, our loved ones do not choose to leave us and they certainly don't do so with any bad intentions.

So, when you cry out in frustration, "Why did you do this to me?", quickly calm down and perhaps say a prayer, or recall a special memory to quickly dispel this thought.

MOVING WITH

So often told to just move on,
That your sorrow and grief will
Soon to be gone.

Do not slip into this myth,
for you do not want to move on,
But rather to move WITH

Always WITH the love you shared,
and the memories that showed
How much you cared

Always WITH those who taught you much
Always WITH friends who were always there

Remember always to not just move on, for if
you do all else might be gone

FAMILIAR FACES AND FAMILIAR PLACES

Sooner or later you must begin the return trip into what will become your new normal life.

So, each day your life will be filled with memories as you travel to those ordinary daily stops and encounter the people who were part of what became. "The rhythm of your life".

The places are the most common things one would do. They are the grocery store, gas station, library, bank, drug store and many others. The people are not family, not friends, simply ordinary folks who formed your world.

These places, and most importantly, these people will ease you back to reality as they open wide the memories of your life with a loved one.

Embrace each and every person and place because they will bring back the reality of life for you.

HOUSEKEEPING AFTER LOSING A LOVED ONE

Cautiously I went to the attic; the time had come for it to be emptied. Would I be prepared for this event? Light filtered in through a small window and was complemented by several dim bulbs. I thought to myself, What a mess!

The first box that I opened cast me back in time as I was confronted with childhood toys. Games had been played, adventures shared, and old friends long forgotten. Where had time gone, I mused. Then a wooden box yielded treasure in the form of pictures.

Here was the past captured for me to bring into the future. This was a legacy of love and reminiscence. I wanted to relive those events for they had been such magical times. Faces I had forgotten, places since discarded, now all thrust into my consciousness.

Hidden in the corner, the old decorations from Christmas. What special and joyous times they had been. My senses drifted back in time and I really thought I could hear laughter and smell cookies baking on those cold winter days. Where did all of that time fly, too?

Uncovering piles of old clothes, I could see everyone as they had been. The thought of this made me chuckle. There followed old furniture we had romped on, suitcases that had taken us away to magical places, and so much more.

There followed an inventory of all the beloved keepsakes, jewelry, and other personal items that identified and were the essence of my lost loved one.

I silently finished my task, saddened by what had left my life, but then I paused, as I silently gave thanks for the blessing of these memories.

ASSOCIATED GRIEF

This is a type of grief that comes at you from unexpected and surprising sources. You may receive a phone call, note a news article or see something on the internet that instantly causes you to experience grief.

It may be the passing of a beloved public figure, the suffering of unknown people caught unexpectedly by an accident, act of violence or some natural disaster.

Whatever it might be, you can momentarily experience the true and full impact of grief. How long it lasts differs in every instance, but it does pass and generally does not leave any scars.

It is perfectly normal to experience this type of grief and you may take comfort in knowing that it is your Human Nature reacting in a very normal manner.

"We should never underestimate the powerful draw of a bond With a living being that loves us unconditionally, asking very little in return. Losing this comfort and source of joy can be incomprehensible."

– Linda Lipshultz

OUR NON-HUMAN LOVED ONES

So often in our lives we are fortunate enough to enjoy the love, comfort and protection of an animal. But sadly, as with our human loved ones, they pass away.

I am certain the grief that follows such an event can be no less intense than that experienced when you lose a human loved one.

Your animal friend has devoted its life giving you unconditional Love. It has provided you with comfort during illness and It has been a faithful companion during your lonely times. Needless to say, this loss can be a devastating event.

So, grieve unconditionally and wear your grief openly when you experience this kind of loss. Love the memories your animal friend left with you. Remember your laughter during playful times, warmth when they comforted you. Most of all, know they expected nothing more from you than your love and care.

"To Live In Hearts We Leave Behind Is Not To Die."

– Thomas Campbell

NOT THE END, JUST THE BEGINNING

I sincerely hope these words have served to give you some measure of comfort and encouragement.

I urge you to not remain silent in your loss and grief, but rather to embrace the joy and peace that will live on forever in your heart and memory as you navigate through this loss in your life.

Be happy, share and talk to anybody you can about the life of your loved one. Seek a group, a religious source or trusted friend who can accompany you on your journey down your special new road.

You do not have to be lonely or alone on your journey. You will find peace!

My goal in preparing this work is to lift the veil of darkness that surrounds grief. Grief is a real event that occurs naturally and is part of the human experience.

It should not simply be a sad and dark moment, but rather a joyful experience which carries us from one moment in life into the next.

It is our reminder of a life well lived and forever remembered with joy.

ABOUT THE AUTHOR

A graduate of Georgetown University, John A. Kessler has spent more than 35 years in Corporate Human Resources. He has also been a speaker for the American Management Association and has taught evening programs at Fairfield University and Western Connecticut State University.

He is the author of several books, including "Reflections of An Ordinary Person," "Reflections in Poetry," "That's Life" and "Ready, Aim, Retire."

John's mission, which he hopes to accomplish through his writing, is to communicate Hope, Peace and Self-Fulfillment to his readers.

.

www.ingramcontent.com/pod-product-compliance
Lightning Source LLC
Chambersburg PA
CBHW051559120626
46551CB00013B/1590